MY FIRST LOOK AT COUNTRIES

A PICTURE OF ISRAEL'S CITY OF JERUSALEM

Israel

ADELE RICHARDSON

CREATIVE EDUCATION

Published by Creative Education

123 South Broad Street, Mankato, Minnesota 56001

Creative Education is an imprint of The Creative Company

Designed by Rita Marshall

Photographs by Getty Images (Jon Arnold, Richard Ashworth, Gary Cralle, Chuck Fishman, Will & Deni McIntyre, David Silverman, James L. Stanfield, Travel Ink Photo Library, Visual Photo Library, Maynard Owen Williams)

Printed in the United States of America

Library of Congress Cataloging-in-Publication Data

Richardson, Adele, 1966- Israel / by Adele Richardson.

p. cm. — (My first look at countries)

Includes index.

ISBN-13 : 978-1-58341-447-7

I. Israel—Juvenile literature. I. Title.

DS 118R4862 2006   956.94—dc22   2005051777

First edition 9 8 7 6 5 4 3 2 1

ISRAEL

In the Middle East

Israel is a small country. It is part of the **continent** called Asia. Israel is in the southwest part of Asia. Southwest is the bottom left part of Asia on a map. The area is also called the "Middle East."

Israel touches four other countries. It also touches lots of water. Most of the west, or left, side of Israel touches water. A small part of the bottom of Israel touches water, too.

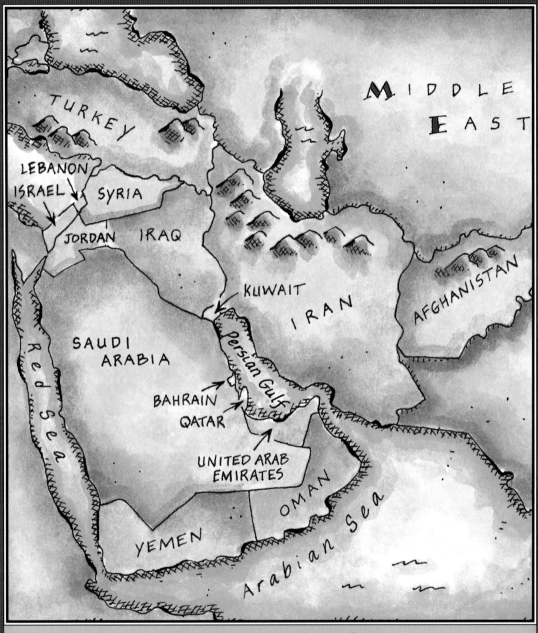

A MAP SHOWING THE MIDDLE EAST

Summer in Israel is hot and dry. Not much rain falls. The north, or top, part of Israel has cool winters. That is when most of the rain falls.

LAND AND SEAS

Israel has lots of mountains and hills. Sometimes it snows in the mountains. But it does not snow most other places in Israel.

People in Israel's deserts
often get around on
the backs of camels.

There are two seas in Israel. The Sea of Galilee is in the north part of Israel. The Dead Sea is near the middle of Israel. The Jordan River links the two seas.

Desert covers the south, or bottom, part of Israel. Few trees grow in the desert. But some people try to grow plants there. They grow fruits such as strawberries. They build long pipes to bring water for the plants!

The salt of the Dead Sea

is very thick. It

makes people float.

ISRAEL'S WILD SIDE

Lots of animals live in Israel. Foxes, hedge-hogs, and frogs live there. Snakes and lizards live there, too.

Lots of **species** of birds live in Israel. Owls and storks live there. So do falcons. Some birds live in Israel all year. Others live there only in the winter.

SOME PEOPLE IN ISRAEL RAISE DONKEYS

The ibex lives in Israel's deserts. It is a large kind of goat. The ibex has long, curved horns. It leaps around in rocky places.

Israel has lots of preserves. Preserves are safe places for animals. People cannot bother the animals in a preserve. They can only look at them.

IBEX LIVE IN SOME OF ISRAEL'S PRESERVES

THE HOLY LAND

Many people call Israel the "Holy Land." That is because many **religions** started there. The religions called Christianity (*Kris-chee-AN-i-tee*) and Islam started in Israel. So did the religion called Judaism (*JOO-day-iz-um*).

Judaism is also called the Jewish religion. Most people in Israel are part of the Jewish religion. They are called Jews.

Jerusalem is the biggest
city in Israel. There is a
wall around part of it.

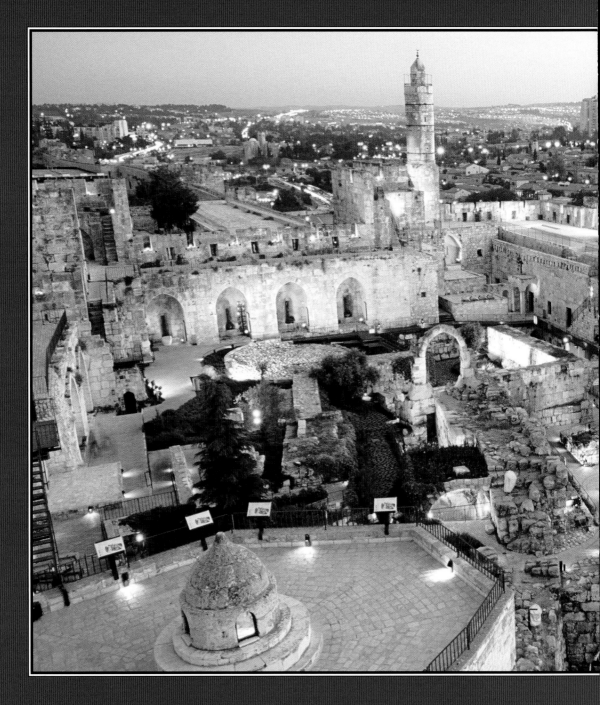

JERUSALEM IS AN OLD, BEAUTIFUL CITY

There are lots of **holidays** in Israel. Schools are closed for holidays. Grown-ups stay home from work.

Passover is a big holiday for Jews. People make special foods for Passover. They sing songs and pray. They spend time with their family and friends. Everyone has lots of fun!

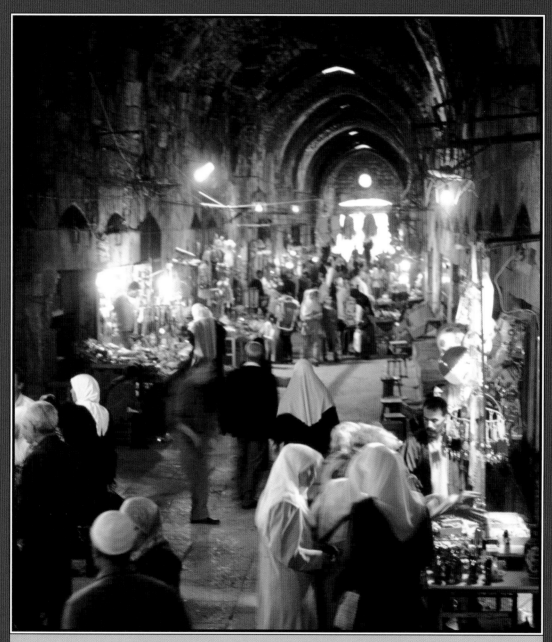

MANY PEOPLE IN ISRAEL HAVE FUN SHOPPING

Hands-on: A Very Salty Sea

The Dead Sea is very salty. It has nine times more salt than ocean water. Here is a way to find out how salty that is!

What You Need

Two eight-ounce (235 ml) glasses of water
A teaspoon
Salt

What You Do

1. Put one teaspoon of salt in the first glass.
2. Pour nine teaspoons of salt into the other glass.
3. Stir the first glass.
4. Stir the second glass.
5. Dip a finger in each glass. Take a small taste of each. Which one is saltier?

SALT FROM THE DEAD SEA COVERS THESE ROCKS

Index

Words to Know

continent—one of Earth's seven big pieces of land

deserts—dry, sandy areas where few plants and trees grow

holidays—special days that happen every year

religions—kinds of beliefs

species—kinds of plants or animals

Read More

Fontes, Justine and Ron. *Israel*. New York: Children's Press, 2004.

Schroeder, Holly. *Israel ABCs: A Book About the People and Places of Israel*. Minneapolis: Picture Window Books, 2004.

Spengler, Kremena. *Israel: A Question and Answer Book*. Mankato, Minn.: Fact Finders, 2005.

Explore the Web

Akhlah: The Jewish Children's Learning Network http://www.akhlah.com

Israel4Kids http://www.israelemb.org/kids/index.html

Virtual Israel http://www.babaganewz.com/virtual